THE OLDE HOUSE AT IPSWICH:

SAVING THE MOSES JEWETT HOUSE

Prudence Paine Fish

The Olde House at Ipswich:
Saving the Moses Jewett House

ISBN: 979-8986017280

All Rights Reserved © 2026 by Richard Fish
No part of this book may be reproduced or transmitted in any form or by any means, graphic, electronic, or mechanical, including photocopying, recording, taping, or by any information storage or retrieval system, without the written permission of the publisher.

Published by Andrew Joyce
Edited by Emily Gmitter

The Moses Jewett House 1850

The Moses Jewett House 1900

The Moses Jewett House 1980

CONTENTS

PART ONE
BACKGROUND

Names on a Mailbox	1
Jewett History	3
Deeds	5
Waiting	6

PART TWO
RESTORING THE HOUSE

Day One	9
Decisions! Decisions! Accommodating an Old House	18
Crews and Consultants	21
The Frontispiece of a House	22
The Cellar Attic and Systems	31
The New Kitchen	34
The Colonial Kitchen	39
Modern Amenities (Kitchen, Baths and Laundry)	41
The Dining Room	43
The Hall	49
The Parlor	50
The Master Bedroom	51
Guest Rooms	52
Rear Rooms on the Second Floor	53
One Bedraggled Barn	54

PART THREE
FINISHED AT LAST

Party Time	59
Incidents Along the Way	61
The Furniture	64
Subdivision	65
Buyers at Last	66
Mistakes	68
Conclusion	69
Post Script	70
Bonus Chapter	71

THE OLDE HOUSE AT IPSWICH:

SAVING THE MOSES JEWETT HOUSE

Part One

Background

NAMES ON A MAILBOX

In 1971, I and my family (husband Dick, children Nancy, Rick and Bob, and our dog, Cinnamon) moved from Connecticut to a new home in Newburyport, Massachusetts. It wasn't new in the sense that it was newly constructed. The house was built in 1800, and the adventure of living in a fourteen-room, Federal-period mansion on High Street at the time of Newburyport's rebirth was exciting, indeed.

Love of old houses was not new to me. My mother had endowed me with that passion, but I had never lived in an antique house. I knew this would be fun.

We still owned our second home in Lanesville on Cape Ann and continued to spend summers there. That meant countless trips back and forth between the two houses, a fifty-minute trip.

I could not complain. It was a lovely drive. Past the antique shops of Essex I drove, on to the farms of Ipswich, then passing the Old Green in Rowley and the Newbury marshes and up to the Parker River, which marked the entrance to Newbury's Lower Green, next to the Upper Green, until I finally arrived at beautiful High Street. There was always something to look at. The trip included frequent detours around Ipswich to look at the old houses and absorb New England at its best. I loved it all.

The Olde House with the Aluminum Awning

One house always caught my eye. It sat by itself amidst overgrown fields, shabby with an aluminum awning above the front door. A rickety barn, barely upright, was holding on for dear life at the end of the sweeping driveway. In better days, someone had painted its construction date prominently on the chimney … 1759.

After absorbing this forlorn scene, my eyes would always catch sight of the mailbox on the side of the road near the end of the driveway. On it was painted two names: Orcutt and Waycott. *What a tongue twister*, I thought. As I drove along, I would think, *Was it Orcott and Waycutt or was it Orcutt and Waycott?* until I wasn't sure anymore. I mused that I would have to look at it again the next time I drove by. My brain went through this silly exercise with each trip. How could two names in one house be so alike but different? Were these families related?

Fast forward to 1981. Ten years have passed. I have now embarked on a new real estate career working in Ipswich, drawn to that town by the early houses. Living in Newburyport had advanced my love of old houses, my knowledge, and my research skills.

One day, with no warning, two associates, David Martin and Tony Watters, came into the office and said, "Ya' know that old house up toward Rowley with 1759 on the chimney? Well, Mr. Waycott died and it is for sale to settle his estate. Tony and I are thinking of buying it and fixing it up on spec. It has six acres of land. Want to go in with us?"

What! Me? That Waycott-Orcutt house? Tell me more!

The only one living in the house was Wayne Orcutt. The house needed lots of work but it was only $79,000, including all that land.

There must be potential in this deal, I thought. So I agreed. The three of us added another partner, Vernon Martin, and put the old place under agreement. Our lawyer explained that in the case of an estate settlement the property goes to the highest bidder. Even with a signed Purchase and Sales Agreement, the estate is not bound. Another buyer could come in with a higher offer at the last minute and it would be all over. We must close as quickly as possible. There were other interested buyers.

We looked the house over. Yuk! Everything smelled like mildew. Was it the hay that had been banked around the foundation for so long? Was it the network of streams running through the cellar floor?

Tattered curtains and pulpy wallpaper made the rooms depressing. The furnishings were overstuffed, mostly non-descript and decrepit. The fireplaces were covered. There was one miserable bathroom upstairs with a claw foot tub and a half bath downstairs in the lean-to. Neither was worth saving. The lean-to was tipping away from the house! The windows were rattling and in collapse. There were radiators and an old, heavy gas stove that dominated the kitchen. And we mustn't forget the barn. There's nothing more depressing than an unrestored antique house. In the process of restoration, "it gets worse before it gets better."

All in all, it was the perfect picture of a rundown old New England farmhouse and we were naïve buyers. What we lacked in smarts we made up for in enthusiasm.

The closing was set for the first week in September, 1981. Fall would be a nice time to work on the house. I was about to set out on the greatest learning experience of my life. On that day, my relationship with the Waycott-Orcutt place (I finally got it straight) began. Nearly a third of a century has passed and the relationship continues. It has been more than forty years since I first became fixated on a dilapidated old house with a past, a future, and strange names on its mailbox, and forty years since my knowledge of old houses was seriously tested.

JEWETT HISTORY

While nervously awaiting the closing, there were plans to make and things to do. My first stop was the Registry of Deeds in Salem where I researched the chain of title back to Moses Jewett.

The Jewett farm was originally the Muzzy farm. The homestead was near the great spring on the Egypt River. It was an isolated location way off the highway. Muzzy moved to Newbury in the vicinity of Marlborough Street, formerly called Muzzy's Lane. Today that location is in Newburyport. Muzzy sold his farm of about 100 acres to Joseph Jewett, who was already a landowner of note in 1654.

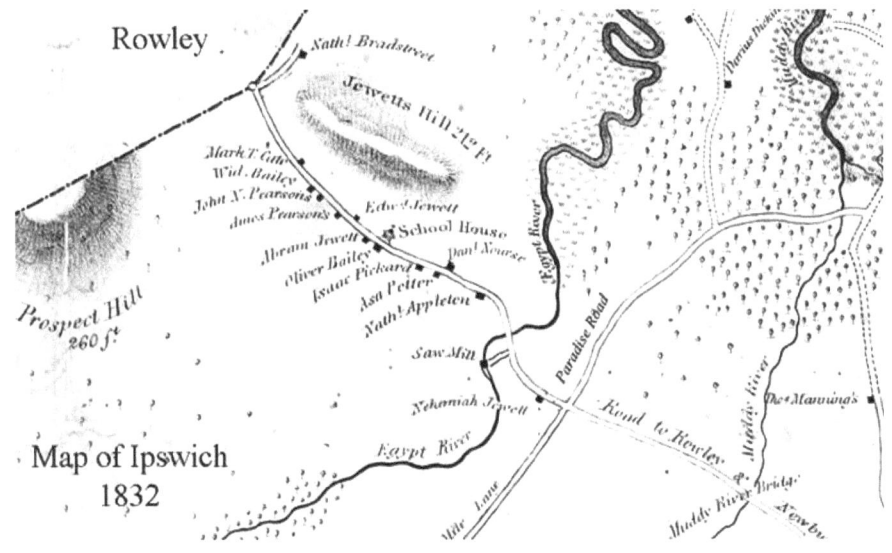

When Joseph Jewett died in 1660, his estate included a new house and barn. Each generation that followed further divided the land. The next generation on the land was Jeremiah Sr., then Jeremiah Jr., followed by Aaron and finally Moses, the builder of our house, at least the second if not the third house to be built on this large farm.

In 1741, Moses Jewett married Abigail Bradstreet, the "girl next door" but more accurately the girl from the next farm. They had a total of ten children, five girls and five boys. During the Revolution, Moses served in Gloucester with a horse troop protecting Gloucester Harbor, as did his son, Aaron.

Aaron built his house up the road about 1780, and succeeding generations did likewise until there was (and still is) a string of Jewett houses along that stretch of road representing the homesteads of numerous generations of Jewetts from the 18th to the 20th centuries.

Aaron was born in 1744. He married Hannah Pearson from the neighborhood in 1769. They lived in the house that Aaron built on land given to him by his father, Moses. Their house was not unlike the house that Moses built; both typical country architecture of the Georgian period with large center chimneys.

In 1793, Aaron's wife, Hannah, died. She had hanged herself in the cellar. She was soon discovered, but not soon enough to save her. Aaron and Hannah had eight children.

A year later, on November 8, 1794, Moses' wife, Abigail, passed away at 72. Her stone in the Rowley cemetery records this plaintive verse.

> *The rising morning can't insure*
> *That we shall end the day;*
> *For death stands ready at the door*
> *To take our lives away.*

Aaron and Moses both served in the Revolutionary War. Moses was Captain of a troop of horse (a cavalry unit). Aaron was a private in his father's horse troop when they marched on the alarm of April 19, 1775. They got as far as Medford but missed the action at Lexington. Again on November 29, 1775, Captain Moses Jewett and his son, Aaron, now a corporal, marched to Gloucester. In 1796, Capt. Moses Jewett died. He was 75 years old. His probate listed his occupation as "Gentleman."

Just prior to Moses' death, Aaron had married Elizabeth Bradstreet from the neighboring farm. Aaron then inherited his father's house and made that his home for the rest of his life. Aaron and Elizabeth had two children, Amos and Eliza. Aaron died in 1824 and Elizabeth in 1834. The former Aaron Jewett house now became known as the Cate house. Aaron's daughter, Eliza, had married Mark French Cate and the house Aaron Jewett built became their home.

After their deaths, Amos Jewett, a grandson, began to sell off parts of the property to Daniel Boynton.

DEEDS

The deeds revealed that the house had now been divided into two houses. The west or left side of the house was sold in 1835 with a "line to the center of said house on the back side, thence through the middle of said dwelling house to the front side thereof." In 1844, the east side was sold to Daniel Boynton, this time from front to back. "Northeasterly through the center of the front entry and center of the chimney of said dwelling house to the back side of said house." Yet another deed referenced the chimney and the kitchen fireplace. That's how we knew a fireplace existed somewhere in the house, although there was no visible evidence.

The old house next descended by inheritance to Warren Boynton, then to Fannie Smith (1913), Emily Wilson (1917), and Charles Gunn (1921). Charles Gunn sold to Edgar Eilenberger (1926). It next descended to Greta Eilenberger Waycott and her husband, William Raymond Waycott (1953), from whom we bought it.

The Ipswich library has yearbooks representing the Jewett Family of America. One yearbook traced their ancestry all the way back to Adam and Eve. Yikes!

Franklin Waters described this old farm in his book, *Ipswich Village and the Old Rowley Road*. Ipswich Village was a hamlet whose residents did all their trading in Rowley and attended the Rowley church. In fact, Ipswich Village wanted to secede from Ipswich and become part of Rowley, but Ipswich wouldn't let them go. Ipswich wanted their taxes. There were several failed attempts as the people of the village attempted this separation.

One of the old deeds referred to the highway as the Post Road. Taking that name, we formed a corporation called Post Road Development Corporation. We chose Paul Leone from Merrimacport as general contractor. I don't know who recommended him to us, but it was a choice we never regretted for a split second.

WAITING

The scope of work grew and grew. Sills were rotted all the way around; the dining room sill had rolled because its supporting wall had buckled.

The entire heating system, boiler and radiators, had to go, as did all other plumbing of every sort.

All electrical was to be removed, including old BX cable as well as knob and tube wiring. There was a severe water problem evident in the cellar. What to do about that?

The chimney was crumbling. The flashing around the chimney was leaking into the attic with big black streaks on the chimney. There were no fireplace dampers and no hearths.

The kitchen, bathrooms, and laundry would have to be redone from scratch; all except the 2nd-floor bathroom would also need to be relocated.

The circa 1840 Greek revival front door and surround had to go. The driveway, front walkway, and grounds were a mess. The plaster was tired; the lumpy ceilings reminded me of oatmeal. The essential back staircase had been removed.

PART TWO
RESTORATION BEGINS

DAY ONE

The day for passing papers arrived quickly but none too fast for our little group of investors. With great excitement we drove to Peabody to complete the transaction.

After dressing appropriately for the closing, I packed a change of clothing… old clothing. I couldn't wait to get my hands on that old house and I knew it was going to be messy.

Furthermore, I had made a side deal with the sellers. I had purchased the remaining contents of the house for $300. My scheme was as follows. After sorting out the junk, the salable items would be sold in Bob Molinski's shop: Ipswich Used Furniture on Central Street. Furniture needing refinishing or repairs would be handled by our daughter, Nancy Fish, and then sold at Bob's. Nancy and I would split the proceeds from those items. Later, the enormous, overstuffed chairs were dragged out onto the grass in front of the house where they lay on their sides looking like great prostrated behemoths or, as David might have said, "beached whales."

After the formalities in Peabody, we almost ran to our respective cars and headed north to Ipswich. As I pulled into Ipswich, I made a quick stop at Agawam Hardware to purchase a hammer. Who knew what kind of demolition tools we would need before this day was over?

Roses Through Tattered Curtains

It was a perfect day. Not a cloud in the sky. The weather was pleasant. Old, sweet-smelling pink roses were blooming around the house, and the big hydrangea was ready to blossom.

We walked around the property. In the field behind the barn, someone had been growing gourds. They lay there in all their glory, in the bright sunlight, the epitome of autumn and harvest. In back of the barn were beehives. But we could not linger long out-of-doors. We needed to move on and get acquainted with the ancient, moldy heap that was now ours.

Endangered Barn

The golden rod is yellow. The corn is turning brown.
The fields and apple orchards. With fruit are bending down.
With all these lovely tokens September days are here.
With summer's best of weather and autumn's best of cheer.
        —Helen Hunt Jackson, 1902

Before going inside, however, David and Tony were determined to remove the aluminum awning from over the front door. That had to go in a hurry, putting the world on notice that things were changing at the old Waycott-Orcutt house. A hornet's nest in the awning slowed the work only momentarily.

Overgrown

The three of us attacked the house, making holes everywhere. Our immediate quest was for hidden fireplaces and paneling. Within the hour, there were piles of plaster and debris everywhere. What a mess we had made in so short a time! Meanwhile, Tony's wife, Dianna, was taking slides to record the scene.

The object of our greatest attention was the area of the colonial kitchen. Remember the deed that had indicated a fireplace of which there was no trace?

Allow me to take you on a journey of discovery.

We disconnected the large stove, dragged it aside, and began to demolish the wall behind the spot where it had been connected with a pipe into the chimney and where we thought there should be a fireplace. The demolished remains of wood lath and plaster began to pile up.

We then noticed a moldy smell, but that was traced to a wet trunk of rotted material in the cellar.

Making a Mess

It's hard to believe that the ten foot fireplace was on the left behind all of this clutter and confusion.

The Old Stove is Disconnected and the Debris Piles Up Quickly

Eventually we broke through all the layers and found a bricked-up, filled-in fireplace opening. There was the fireplace we were anticipating, right where we expected. It had an oven way in the back, the sign of an early fireplace, along with the expected straight jambs and oak lintel.

We finished the excavation. Although the features were correct, the proportions were strange. It was an extremely tall fireplace but not as wide as expected. Something about it was a little off. The proportions weren't right. I tried to act excited, but inside I felt an uncomfortable twinge of disappointment. In truth, it was a let-down and not the fabulous walk-in fireplace I had dared to anticipate.

After shining a light up the chimney, David announced from inside the firebox that the brick wall on the right side terminated up above his head in the big throat of the chimney. A few bricks were knocked off little by little with great apprehension. Were we doing the right thing or wrecking the fireplace? Soon, David was standing on a mountain of bricks and mortar on the fireplace floor. Then more and more courses of brick were knocked off until David, who was working inside the fireplace (Tony and

I were outside), was able to scramble over the top of this brick wall into another duplicate fireplace with an identical second oven; a mirror image of the first fireplace! What was going on? The answer was in the old deed! We had bought the divided house complete with a divided cooking fireplace…one half for each family.

While Tony and I worked from the room, David started working his way out from his dark cell. When we finally broke through and David escaped, he found himself in a closet created during the Victorian period when the fireplace was no longer used.

Remains of the Closet in Front of the Fireplace

Much more demolition was needed to remove the closet, an adjoining hallway, and to reattach the small den to the rest of the old kitchen of which it had once been a part. Evidence suggested that it was the former location of the back stairs and buttery.

Now we could begin to imagine what an incredible fireplace we had discovered.

As the dust cleared and the mountains of debris were shoveled away, we took a good look. Eureka! A walk-in fireplace of enormous proportions with two large beehive ovens staring back at three happy restorers. What a bonanza. This huge fireplace, a few inches shy of ten feet in width, rivals the best and biggest 18th century fireplaces in New England. Our gamble that we would find a cooking fireplace exceeded our wildest expectations. Perhaps the size of the huge arched chimney base in the cellar should have been a clue that we were in for a surprise, but I guess we were too naïve to think about such an outcome from our first adventure in excavation.

Smaller holes with less destruction gave us confidence that the house was very intact. Paneling was evident in the four front rooms, and feather-edged sheathing covered all of the interior walls of the rear rooms. Most of it had never been painted, sealed away for at least one hundred fifty years.

It got better and better, but a new problem was emerging. Our "spec" house for a quick pick-me-up and resale revealed itself to be a serious antique in serious condition; a dilapidated chunk of Ipswich history with all of its pieces and parts intact but hidden. We had to make some weighty decisions relative to our next steps. We were naïve but learning about ancient houses and restoration in a crash course. At least we had enough knowledge to recognize, in spite of its physical condition, that we had a house that deserved the most expert decisions of which we were capable.

Not that it wasn't exciting. It was thrilling. But we needed to step back and regroup. We had to do right by this old house. We had to be restorers all the way, not renovators, remodelers, or worse yet, remuddlers. We shouldn't cut corners. We couldn't compromise this landmark that Post Road Development Corporation now owned. Decisions would be harder to make, research would be needed. Getting it right was essential, but would cost more. Could we make it a financial success? We certainly hoped so. What had we done?

Compounding the dilemma was the awareness that we had no idea who the buyer would be. That meant keeping salability in mind. We needed to find a balance that would satisfy the purest but not inhibit appeal to a more general audience and marketplace. It had to be good, well-done, but not become an old house museum. It would need nice baths and a nice kitchen with good equipment.

We would have to be very careful and research each decision. I took this assignment very seriously.

DECISIONS! DECISIONS!
ACCOMODATING AN OLD HOUSE

Early in the process, we decided that it would be best to accommodate the house. And that remained my motto: *Accommodate the old house instead of trying to make the old house accommodate you.* That meant working with the house and what it was, a mid-18th century antique. That also meant not removing original fabric, enlarging spaces or cutting up existing spaces. We would be committed to working within the confines of the existing house. It would be a challenge to find solutions and a way around obstacles in order to achieve the desired result…a carefully restored house that looked like the 18th century, but functioning as a 20th century house should function.

To make the house accommodate us would have meant loss of integrity and a heavy-handed approach with loss of the original fabric. No, we would overcome these challenges.

Initially, we thought that the colonial kitchen with its almost ten-foot fireplace would make a super family kitchen. At our first meeting with our general contractor, Paul Leone, we discussed the kitchen layout. At some point in the discussion, Paul suggested that the sink should go over near the windows. I stared at the cavernous fireplace, authentic and original, and then tried to picture the stainless steel sink on the opposite wall. Something in my brain snapped at that moment and screamed, "No!" This marvelous, wonderful, ancient room could not be a 20th century kitchen. No way!

And so that plan was abandoned. The kitchen would go in a restored 19th century lean-to. In order to integrate the proposed kitchen with what would become the antique kitchen/family room, we decided to enlarge the door openings between the two spaces so that the two rooms could communicate better with each other.

The Lean-to Would Become a Working Kitchen

On the plus side, it dawned on us that by changing the plan we were relegating bath, kitchen and laundry to the less important added-on lean-to, leaving the original rooms pure and free from 20th century equipment that goes with a working house. This was a good thing.

Only the bath on the second floor invaded the authentic space, and that bath would be relegated to the space occupied by the existing old bath. No new space would be borrowed or created.

The two exterior doors on the rear of the lean-to had previously been the back door entrances for different rooms when the house was divided. Both would remain. The first would be the working back door closest to the driveway. The second would give access to the downstairs bath or a direct route to the back stairs without crisscrossing the working area of the kitchen. Thus, the fenestration and doors on the rear of the house would remain untouched, and the two doors would be an asset, especially for a family.

Two Doors on the Rear Would Work for a Family's Traffic Pattern

This process of working through a myriad of problems without disturbing anything sensitive became our mission. We even planned light switches to be as inconspicuous as possible in the period rooms, but in a nod toward modern times, installed plenty of electrical outlets near the windows to accommodate window lights at Christmas!

Looking back, I like to think we were as respectful and sensitive as practicality and budget would allow.

THE CREW AND CONSULTANTS

Our general contractor—the thoughtful, efficient, Paul Leone—was always on top of every detail, along with the subcontractors for wiring, heating, and plumbing. Materials were always there in advance, and the project moved forward in an orderly progression under Paul's supervision. Coordination and scheduling were flawless.

To restore the chimney, fireplaces, and missing hearths, Paul brought in Richard Irons. How lucky we were! Today, some thirty years later, Richard is recognized as the master in his field and is still a good friend.

Paul McGinley, an Ipswich resident with a great resume in the preservation field, spent time with us discussing possible appropriate scenarios. Paul is also still a good friend.

My dear departed friend, Nellie Meras from Exeter, New Hampshire, responded to my call for help with color, paint, wallpapers, and general decorating and cosmetic issues. None of us ever forgot her excellent advice, repeated often when we were struggling to pick out a color: "Now remember," she would warn us, "intensity increases with volume," if she thought we were getting too carried away with a questionable color. Whenever we had a request for more paint, especially a color she mixed herself called "tusk," she would immediately respond with, "I'll be right over the road and bring it to you. And then we'll go out for coffee…on me." And come she did in her little green wagon, many, many times. Nellie has long since passed on, but her words of advice still echo in my ears and her friendship is a fond memory.

Daughter, Nancy Fish, helped with paint stripping and scraping. She was a genius at staining and matching colors where repairs had been made, blending the finishes until the repairs became invisible. She also worked feverishly to rejuvenate the furniture I had purchased from the estate to make it salable in Bob's shop.

Son Bob Fish and Donn Pollard were ever present, day after day; helping hands, doing a little of everything. During breaks, David taught Bob to play the guitar.

Our handy man, Dick Mackey, along with his helpers, carted off junk including old plumbing, the boiler and radiators. He knew a little bit about everything and hung around a lot, offering valuable advice. He was interesting and very useful, and he knew antiques like no one else.

Rodney Barrett, an old friend and skilled carpenter, ambitiously tackled the barn.

Jackie Cordima, a new broker, worked hard to find us a buyer. She showed the house many times to prospective buyers.

"Teddy the Painter" from Haverhill and his crew of hard-working, non-English-speaking, Greek immigrants prepared, primed and painted the outside.

One of Dottie Brigham's sons (whose first name I have forgotten) laid the brick walkway.

Cassidy Forge from Rowley provided the Boston post light and door latches. Cassidy designed and made the dining room chandelier, equipped for candles. The dining room would have candles over the table and no electric fixture.

The cast is long and some overlooked, but all did their jobs well.

THE FRONT DOOR AND EXTERIOR

The Moses Jewett house represents the quintessential New England colonial farmhouse, stunning in the snow. It's a textbook example of a Currier and Ives Christmas card scene.

Such houses as these built in the 18th century usually had a five-bay façade; four windows on the first floor with a door in the middle. The second-floor windows were tucked up high under the eaves. The front door entered into a tiny hall (sometimes called the lobby) with a three-run staircase running up in front of the big center chimney. These tiny halls were usually dark, especially with the doors to the front rooms closed for heat conservation as they probably always were.

So it was not surprising that the Greek revival door, in vogue before 1840, took New England by storm. Hundreds of old houses replaced their Georgian doors and surrounds with a new four-panel door and sidelights with panes of glass all the way down to the sill. Such was the scenario with the Jewett house.

A lot of time was devoted to studying Georgian door surrounds in the general area for ideas and inspiration. We didn't know what the original looked like. We could only guess what was originally there, so it was pure conjecture and choice that prompted us. Always liking something with a slightly different twist, I focused on a door with fluted pilasters and a curved pediment instead of the more common Georgian triangular pediment.

As the Greek revival doorway was dismantled, pieces of the original emerged. They had been recycled into the Greek doorway. We found one fluted pilaster that would serve as a prototype for replacements.

When all of the old door and its surround had been removed (including the clapboards in the immediate vicinity), what we found etched in the old sheathing above the door was a curve. This was some indication of what was there originally and a confirmation that our choice was not too far off. That was exciting, and after that discovery there was no question we would reproduce a curved pediment. And we did.

The six-panel door was salvaged from a Gloucester veterans' housing project that had traded in their good, solid pine, six-panel doors for steel doors. Nancy stripped years of paint from the door and applied a new natural finish. The two small panels at the top were removed and replaced with bull's eye panes of glass. These not only looked great, but allowed a little light into the hall. An iron thumb latch and iron door knocker completed the restoration of the all-important front door, the frontispiece of a Georgian house. The opening in the center of the curved pediment has provided a perfect niche for the beautiful, prize-winning Christmas displays created for that spot in the years to come by the next owner, Jerry Bowman.

Traditional Door from a Gloucester Project

Recreating the Georgian Door Surround

A Boston post light was mounted on a substantial post near the new brick walkway leading to the beautiful door.

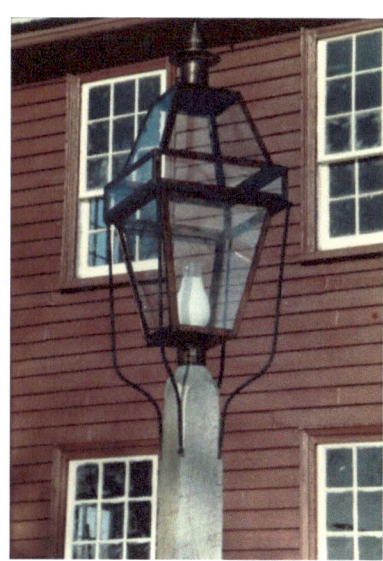

A back entry was ripped off. New wood windows with true divided lights were installed. (The old windows from the 19th century were deemed to be too far gone.) The chimney was repaired and parged. Onion lights from the Bow House in Bolton were installed next to each of the two back doors in the rear of the house. The cellar bulkhead was rebuilt and stone laid on the driveway.

View Out the Kitchen Window

Heave-ho!

View From the Parlor Window

There was another exterior door in the Beverly jog on the left side of the house. The jog was in the 19th century lean-to. The door was restored but permanently locked, and the inside sheetrocked over in order to create wall space for the washer and dryer in the downstairs bath/laundry. We theorized that it would be better to handle the problem this way without the loss of any original fabric. One hundred years from now, if someone has another plan for the house, the change can be reversed and the door re-activated.

Door in the Beverly Jog

Another of my mottos became etched in my brain with that decision: *Do not do anything that can't be reversed.*

It had been decided that the house would be red. It had been white for as long as anyone could remember. Red would take a little getting used to. At some point along the way, in the 19th century, most houses received a fashionable coat of white paint along with green shutters at the windows.

That was the scenario with the Moses Jewett house. Older photos reveal the presence of shutters in the past, but they were long gone. Since they and the white paint more or less represented the 19th century, we opted for an earlier look.

We decided on oil-based paint in Morristown Red, a color available at that time from Benjamin Moore. Teddy the Painter came from Haverhill with his hard-working, smiling Greek workers. The first day, the house was still white as it was scraped. The second day, it was covered with gray primer. The third day, the house was red. If you blinked you might miss a color. Presto chango! They were fast. Everything was painted red except for the window sash. Only they were left ochre yellow. The door was natural.

The result pleased us very much and an early snowstorm presented us with a picture-postcard vision of a house. We all rushed over to see it in the snow and put a wreath on the front door. The house was a show-stopper. We were heady with success. So far so good!

Rodney Barrett took over the work on the barn. This was a huge job and it would cost a lot to save it. We reasoned that an old barn in the country was more acceptable and appropriate with an antique house than a new two-car garage for a similar amount of money. The aesthetic appeal of the old barn with its second story won out. The barn was brought back from the dead and to a fully functional building.

Can This Barn Can Be Saved?

Rodney Barrett Tackles the Restoration of the Barn

The Finished Barn

THE CELLAR, ATTIC, AND SYSTEMS

The least exciting place for me on the whole property was the cellar. Ugh! The floor was a network of trenches running around and across the cellar until they all converged at a hole in the foundation through which a lot of water exited the cellar and found its way to a marshy gully near the house.

This would never do. This was, after all, the 20th century and this system was worse than make-shift, so the floor was cemented, the trenches disappeared, and the hole to the outside was plugged. A sump pump was installed. The cellar was cleaned up, but the sump pump was awfully busy.

The powder post beetle damage was taken care of and the beams scraped of all the damage.

The brick chimney arch was extremely large. It went from side to side. But across the back was another very wide arch supporting the enormous kitchen fireplace.

The Huge Chimney Base

We decided to stay with oil heat. There was gas in the street but not in the house. An old house down the street had just been demolished in a gas explosion and that made me nervous. Plus, at that time oil was cheaper.

We settled on a Weil McLean boiler with a Becket burner. We didn't like hot air, the radiators were gone for good, and that really left hot water baseboard heat as the best if not only option. We reasoned that the more zones, the more efficient the system. We decided that three zones made sense: one for the sleeping area on the second floor, one for the formal rooms (dining room and parlor), and the third zone for the family living area (the kitchen, first floor bath and colonial kitchen/family room). Flexible lengths of copper pipe, a new invention, allowed the piping to go around the big beams without drilling through them to accommodate non-flexible pipes.

Arch Supporting the Cooking Fireplace with Two Ovens

We left a propane gas hot water heater in the cellar so that the new owners would have the option of switching over in the summertime. With the gas hot water heater taking over, the boiler could be shut down in warm weather for economy.

The wiring would be completely new with a 100 amp service (the standard at that time) with circuit breakers.

Moving to the attic, all of the floor boards were removed, thick insulation placed between the joists, and the floor re-laid.

A change was made in the attic staircase: The stairs rose up from a location near the east bedchamber, a somewhat inconvenient access point. There was a closet underneath the attic stairs, opening from another room. By flipping the direction of the stairs, access would be easy from the back stairs. The closet would now be next to the main bedchamber. That arrangement was much more sensible and was easily accomplished with no loss of fabric.

The septic was a cesspool that was working OK. To make it continue to be sufficient, we added a dry well for gray water. This system would no longer be acceptable by today's standards, nor acceptable to a buyer, but at that time it was legal and fine.

Flipping the Attic Stairs Around for Convenience

THE NEW KITCHEN

Now that we had agreed the working kitchen would be in the lean-to, along with the second bath and laundry, we were facing the challenge of creating a kitchen that worked for us both in efficiency and aesthetics. Nellie had drilled it into our heads that there should be a continuity between rooms, an easy flow, and a psychologically pleasing transition of color, style, and materials as one passed from one room to another.

We abandoned our original idea of trendy, contemporary, light-colored laminate cabinets. (In retrospect, how could we ever have considered this?) We now settled on pine cabinets with raised panels that made more sense. Mexican tiles with a charming handmade look covered the wall space between the counters and the overhead cabinets.

Location of Future Kitchen in the Lean-to

Framing the New Bath/Laundry with Loft Above

Work Continues on the Bath/Laundry and Loft

A large multi-paned window was installed at the driveway end of the kitchen where we envisioned a spot for a small table and chairs.

Before

After

The woodwork and floor were pine,. The floor was new by necessity. New floors would be stained and finished with satin urethane. All old floors would be painted. In this way, we tried to please the expected buyer who adores pine floors and also please someone with a somewhat more purist mindset.

This modern kitchen would have a cathedral ceiling, complete with two large Velux skylights. The two back doors also had small panes of glass on the top two-thirds. This kitchen would be bright and sunny.

For appliances, we chose a Jennair stove with convection oven that vented downward. The dishwasher was Maytag, the sink a double stainless steel with a single control faucet. This was before the days when granite and stainless steel would become the standard by which a kitchen would be judged.

Track lighting filled the illumination needs. The counter tops were a neutral Formica. At the far end of the kitchen, we partitioned off a bath/laundry. Above this space was created a loft with a balustrade overlooking the kitchen. Its entrance was from an upstairs room.

The downstairs bath received an imitation quarry tile floor. The pine vanity had a terra cotta Formica counter top. The shower stall was fiberglass.

There were hook-ups for a washer and dryer in front of the sealed-up door in the Beverly jog. Nellie came "over the road" with a small-print wallpaper from Old Stone Mill for the walls.

We maintained the pine of the adjacent area, provided good equipment for 1981, and an easy transition to the next space, the colonial kitchen/family room. This completes a description of our new kitchen.

Best of all we had confined the equipment, appliances and modern functions of a working house to the added lean-to without invading the period rooms. Mission accomplished.

View From the Kitchen Window

THE COLONIAL KITCHEN

Without doubt, the most dramatic room in the house was the old kitchen with its cavernous fireplace. This would become the focal point of this restoration and the important all-purpose room in the house just as it had been in colonial days.

In its original configuration, this area would have been divided into three sections. The evidence was there, but the changes took place long ago, beginning when the house was divided in two. In its original form, approximately one-third of the space at the east end, toward the driveway, would have been the first-floor bedroom. Today people would call it the "borning room," a misnomer and term arising from the colonial revival period, about one hundred years ago. This room was romanticized as a room reserved for childbirth, but in reality it was a bedroom for whatever purpose needed. It was handy to the kitchen fireplace, warmer than the upstairs, and practical for an elderly, sick, lame or other needy family member.

A smaller area at the opposite end of this large space would have been reserved for a buttery and a back stair. The largest space centered in front

39

of the big fireplace, the heart of the colonial period home—the most significant living/working part of the house.

The back staircase was missing, so we had to build a functional staircase in the back for the restoration of the old house to be authentic. In a central-chimney house, the large chimney occupies the middle of the building. The front stairs turn by necessity, allowing access to the two front bedrooms but no direct access to the back half of the house except through the front bedchambers. Therefore, a back staircase accessing these rooms and providing a more convenient direct route to the second floor was imperative.

The carpenters built the staircase leading up to the room in the back. A few more steps across the room accessed the attic door and stairs making it infinitely easier to carry things from the first floor straight to the attic rather than the circuitous route previously called for.

After pulling down plaster on the inside walls of the kitchen, we uncovered much feather-edged casing covering the whole interior wall. The only missing pieces were just above the recently exposed fireplace. A few scraps and remnants of that wall were left and reproduced. Although fireplaces at the period the house was built did not have mantels, we took the liberty of adding a mantel in the old kitchen since there was nothing left from the original to alter. Mantels are nice. They provide a place for a clock, candlesticks, or holiday decorations and were often added to existing paneled walls.

Modern Amenities, Kitchen, Baths & Laundry

There had once been a door from what would become the dining room into the small first-floor bedroom. There was another door that had always led from the future dining room into the old kitchen. In its present state, it left two doors almost side by side connecting the same two spaces. We handled this by covering the door on the dining room side and permanently closing the door on the kitchen side. This change can be reversed at any time in the future. No original fabric was disturbed.

The ceiling was not original at all. There were several layers of squares, bad plaster, and damage from old plumbing. Then we discovered that, in its early years, the ceiling had been whitewashed and not plastered. This was unusual. This was not a first period house. But the evidence was clearly there. Old greasy whitewash clung to the beams and floorboards above. It was dirty, yellowed, and disgusting. But rather exciting to recognize that this second period house—farmhouse that it was—had not had a plastered ceiling for a long time. The absence of split lath indicated that the ceiling came much, much later. So we left the ceiling uncovered after cleaning off the now-offensive whitewash. An open ceiling in a house of this period is not the norm. I would not have expected it, but it seemed important to remain faithful to what we found. People love beamed ceilings, anyway, and we were able to justify its veracity.

A large soil line and other pipes led to the bathroom above. A tidy step-back pine cupboard was built to disguise some pipes, and another was boxed in pine and resembled a vertical post. These offending pipes were neatly disguised.

The biggest issue was the fireplace hearth. There was none left. We had to begin again from scratch.

Richard Irons and his crew set the hearth in place. I objected. It seemed too shallow to balance such a huge fireplace. I imagined the fireplace tipping forward on such a small platform. More courses of bricks were added. I was still not satisfied. Nellie came over the road to the restoration masons and proclaimed, "We have to understand life at that time period. We have to visualize how they lived, how they cooked, spun, did their weaving, candle making, soap making, and socializing, all around the big fireplace." Then she startled the men by saying, "Why, in those days, who knows? They may have even slaughtered a cow on the hearth!"

Meanwhile, I had been impressed with the large hearth at the Paine-Dodge house in Ipswich, down on the edge of the marsh off Jeffries Neck Road. Finding an image of that hearth in a book, and with the help of a magnifying glass, I carefully counted the courses of brick in that hearth and hoped we could do the same. Mr. Irons did not necessarily approve, but I prevailed.

The following day, as the last courses of brick were added to the hearth, one of the masons was heard to say to the other, "Well, do you think this is big enough for your average cow?"

Right or wrong, I loved it. Many years later, I learned that the one I had copied was not authentic. Oh, well. I still love it!

We had discovered early on that, because the cooking fireplace predated the days of swinging cranes, there were brackets in the chimney for a lug pole. A lug pole was a green sapling that would be inserted up in the throat of the chimney and laid to rest on two brackets called lugs. Trammels hung from the lug pole to which pots and kettles were attached. Historically, the lug pole had to be monitored because they eventually burned out and needed to be replaced before a kettle of soup crashed to the hearth. Our masons dutifully replaced the lug pole. It was good for a laugh years later when a chimney sweep was called in and he reported with alarm to the new owners that there was a big stick up in the chimney and he would remove it for them. No! Leave it alone! I'm happy to report it is still there.

At one point, the building inspector appeared and said the kitchen fireplace was not safe because it had an oak lintel. He insisted that we wrap it in sheet metal. This oak lintel, its beveled face toward the fire, had been doing its job without damage for generations. After adding the sheet metal, we observed that the metal didn't even get hot. The old time masons knew what they were doing and I have seldom seen one that had burned during normal use.

A damper was placed on the top of the chimney, with a chain hanging down into the fireplace and fastened to a hook for opening and closing the damper. This works better than having an oversized iron damper in such a large area to struggle with.

From all the changes—walls added and subtracted, stairs removed, hearth removed, and more—the floor was a lost cause. We had to replace it. Here, as in the new kitchen, the floor was stained. Many potential buyers would love it, and those that didn't could always paint it.

When completed, this room worked well with the new kitchen and became the main living area of the restored house. The size of the big room, the size of the fireplace (and the hearth) still leaves visitors in awe.

THE DINING ROOM

Oh, what a scene! Was there hope for this room? Optimism was hard to muster. There was no sign of the fireplace. A blank wall covered with crumbling, tan, plaid wallpaper. We had to excavate again, just as in the kitchen. It was a mess.

Down came the Victorian plaster and lath, down came studs, out came bricks. What a nice surprise to find a rather large firebox with another brick oven in the rear. That meant three large bake ovens in one chimney. It was unexpected that we would find one here. Perhaps this fireplace had been altered to accommodate two families. A hearth was rebuilt and a damper added.

The Mess We Encountered in Determining Where There Should be a Fireplace

Opened Fireplace with Missing Door on Cupboard Above

Above the fireplace was a cupboard minus its door. On the left of the fireplace was the door to the cellar. The door was Victorian; this was a major change.

The cellar door should have been in the front hallway underneath the staircase. We removed the offending door in the dining room. But wait! What about that panel in the attic? We were lucky. It was the missing panel removed when the cellar door was created. It was necessary to find a door for the cupboard but, after finding that, the rest of the fireplace and surround fell into place. That was the fun part. The rest was not fun.

The raised field panels on the fireplace wall ended at the ceiling—cut off mid-way. Something was wrong here. The ceiling must have been lowered. The panels were incomplete. We reasoned the ceiling must have been lowered to cover the summer beam, a frequent solution for hiding the old summer beam when it was no longer aesthetically acceptable. This 1759 house must have summer beams. How could it not?

The ceiling was horrible beyond description, so we tackled the messy job of pulling it down. Two problems emerged immediately. There was no summer beam. There was just a system of large floor joists—beams really, but parallel. That was the first disappointment.

Next, we found that the panels at ceiling height were not complete above the plaster line, but just ended as three-sided panels with no tops. It was original. That seemed strange, to say the least. Even stranger were the two round holes in the newly uncovered raised field panel over the door to the front hallway. What was the purpose of those holes? Obviously they were very old, because the room had been re-plastered and all of the paneling covered probably in the mid-19th century. It wasn't until long after we sold the house that I understood the reason for this "transom panel."

The outside wall on the driveway side had buckled due to a rotted sill, but more particularly, a rotted and rolled sill. The wall had to be torn out to windowsill height and rebuilt starting with a new pressure-treated sill. There was not enough of that wall left to save, so it had to be sheetrocked. The kitchen wall likewise had to be sheetrocked because of the door to the little bedroom that was no more. That had to be covered and made to disappear. And because we had destroyed the ceiling in our quest for the summer beam and panel tops, a new ceiling was in order.

Piles of Plaster in the Dining Room

That was not all. The pine floor was in an awful condition. Some of the boards were paper-thin; the rest were used for repairs elsewhere. A new floor was laid. Like the new floors in the old and new kitchens, it was stained. We hoped it would appeal to the buyers who were not purists enough to like paint.

So all the repairs were made and new materials introduced. It looked like a new room. The ceiling was too smooth and the corners—where they met the walls—too plumb. Perhaps crown molding around the ceiling would take the sting off those sharp edges. Nice old molding was found at Whitey Davis's salvage yard in Salisbury and installed. That helped. We tried to mimic the earliest color, a soft green. The room was looking better. Perhaps the wallpaper Nellie had would look nice. I had planned to use it at my house but decided to donate it to the Moses Jewett house at the last minute. It was a Chinese Chippendale paper. Nellie called it "bird of paradise, tree of life." The formal name of the pattern was Chartwell. Chartwell was manufactured by Thomas Stahan in Chelsea, Massachusetts. The paper matched the paint perfectly and the outcome was pretty. It is still there and still looks good. The present owners have no plans to change it…ever.

*The Finished Dining Room with New Chandelier and
Chartwell Wallpaper by Strahan*

To enhance the integrity of the old house, we chose not to install a chandelier in the dining room. Cassidy Forge made us a chandelier for candles that would hang on a hook over the table. The center was the wooden hub of an old wagon wheel. Branches and cups for the candles were added. It looked great. Unfortunately, the pleasure it gave us was short-lived. The chandelier was stolen, much more about that later.

In order to provide modern illumination, two small eyeball lights were recessed in front of the fireplace and operated by a dimmer. These lights spotlighted the paneled room end and fireplace. The degree of light could be controlled so that it did not compete with the candles. Many people were shocked that I would consider this modern lighting. But it was the right solution.

At last the room had come together and holds its own with the rest of the house. I'm not sure anyone remembers that so much work was done in this part of the house. It all looks compatible, has mellowed with age, and has a patina to match the rest.

Front Wall of the Dining Room

Later, I understood the two holes above the hall door. The answer became apparent when the new owners tried to have dinner parties with a smoking fireplace that didn't draw well. Over a number of years, they tried different ways of building fires: smaller ones, bigger ones, fires in the rear, fires toward the front. They optimistically always claimed to have found the solution only to be driven out in the middle of dinner by smoke, usually on a cold winter's night with the front door and a window open.

Now I understood the holes in the panel over the door. That fireplace had smoked for two hundred years! The holes were to let the smoke out into the hall or out the front door without opening the door from the dining room to the cold hall. This was not a new problem!

Old-time masons knew how to build a fireplace that would draw well. What happened to this fireplace? My theory is that the fireplace was altered long ago. Probably the oven was added. Maybe it had something to do with the various divisions of the divided house. The mason may have done the best he could to accommodate the occupant with a large firebox, a crane and an oven, but the balance and the draft were changed forever. The fireplace smoked then and it smokes now.

The owners have given up trying to make it work and have resorted to a gas log. It looks pretty good, throws heat, and allows for a cheerful fire at a dinner party. I guess it's the only solution there was. The bottom line is: It's another change that can be reversed. This makes it a good thing.

THE HALL

The tiny hall had a three-run "captain's" staircase with a closed string ascending to the second floor. It wound up tightly against the chimney from left to right. Halfway up the stairs, a fairly large door opened into a closet in the chimney. Closets such as this are not all that common, but are seen occasionally. Aaron Jewett's house just up the street, now belonging to the Stevens family, had a similar closet in the chimney.

The panel under the stairs was reopened to its original use as a cellar door. Again, as in the antique kitchen, we discovered a white-washed ceiling under newer plaster. We allowed the unfinished ceiling to be exposed.

The woodwork was painted with Nellie's "tusk," a versatile gray/green/tan color. For the walls we chose Katzenbach and Warren's "Charles the Third" wallpaper from the Williamsburg collection.

Door Into the Chimney Closet in Stairwell

It was extravagant but a wonderful paper for an early setting. Tin sconces added near the front door and a tin hall light hanging from the second floor ceiling completed the hall restoration. These tin lights, which were authentic copies, came from a very special store much loved and now missed by house restorers: the Federal Street Lighthouse in Newburyport.

One incident in particular stands out. A neighbor and Jewett descendant stopped to see what we were doing. David was on a ladder wallpapering the hall stairwell. David paused for a moment and said, "How come Wayne Orcutt looks so much like Mr. Waycott?" The neighbor pointed her finger in David's face and said, "You just keep hanging that wallpaper." Then she quickly exited the house. *Hmmm ... What was all that about?*

THE PARLOR

The parlor actually needed much less work than the dining room. After we destroyed the dining room ceiling, we were told by Paul they could save all of the plaster and they did. No more ceilings or plaster were removed except where Victorian lath and plaster had to be removed in order to reveal original paneling or sheathing.

The plaster was saved in the parlor. The fireplace was opened and a new hearth built. A damper was put in and the fireplace was ready to go—after Richard Irons had created a new furnace flue in the back space in the center of the huge chimney.

The paneling here was naïve. It was a mixture of raised field paneling and feather-edged sheathing. There was a cupboard above the fireplace just as there had been in the dining room.

The floor was comfortable—worn but salvageable. The woodwork was painted a slate blue and the floor a harmonizing color. The walls were left bone white.

No special or unusual problems were encountered here. That was a break. The restoration of the first floor was complete!

THE MASTER BEDCHAMBER

At the top of the stairs, a turn to the left brings you into the master bedchamber, as it would have been called in the 18th century. Here was a major problem.

As described previously, the back staircase had been removed leaving the front stairs the only access to the second floor. The chimney in the middle necessitated going through one of the front rooms to get to a back room. This would not be an acceptable arrangement for a late-20th-century buyer.

To overcome this problem, an owner in the distant past had found the easiest solution. He divided the bedroom. Three quarters of the space toward the gable end of the house became the bedroom. The remaining one quarter closest to the stairs and chimney was partitioned off creating a corridor running from the front to the back of the house. In this corridor was the paneled fireplace wall with bricked up fireplace and non-existent hearth that should have been in a wonderful room.

This wall would have to be removed to restore the room to its original look. Now that there would be a new back staircase, there was no need for the offending corridor in which was found the best and most sophisticated paneling in the house.

With great care, Paul's crew removed the added wall without destroying the ceiling. I didn't think this could be done, but it was. The entire ceiling was saved, and the floor to which the partition had been nailed was also brought back without damage. The fireplace and hearth were restored and a damper added.

The room was then painted a lovely blue, the floor was painted and the room returned to its original look very carefully and completely. What a beautiful room!

THE GUEST ROOM

The room opposite the master bedchamber—designated as the master bedchamber because it had the best paneling—was another room of similar size. There were no special issues to deal with here. There was a lot of feather-edged sheathing on the fireplace wall and a paneled door at the left of the fireplace, opening to a cupboard. The floor had particularly wide boards and the center had never been painted. There was ancient linoleum and the border around the linoleum had been painted many times. The floor was severely pitched away from the chimney that was holding it up, in the direction of the gable end of the house where the sill had rotted. Leveling this floor would have been much too invasive and result in loss of plaster. It was left alone, hoping that antique buyers would understand and find it acceptable. Lovers of old houses have to have a certain amount of tolerance for the idiosyncrasies that go with an ancient building.

The major problem we had with this room was of our own making. I had seen a color I particularly liked. It was a lovely salmon color. I painted the room with it, and as it dried, it got worse and worse. We tried again. It was almost hot pink! Oh, my gosh. *Help*! Again, Nellie reminded us, "Intensity increases with volume." We should have heeded her advice—I thought it was burned into our brains. We should have had her mix the paint!

We dubbed the room the "bubble gum room" because no matter how hard we tried or how many times we repainted, it always came out looking like bubble gum.

Searching for the right color, I liked what I saw on a chart for Old Village Paints. This was a little different. We had to purchase a can of brownish paint, then a can of off-white, and mix the two together. Voila! A perfectly wonderful, soft salmon emerged as this strange concoction was blended. On the woodwork it looked even better. The bubble gum room was finally history and a lovely, warm, cheerful room was a sight for sore eyes. The bubble gum nightmare was over but never forgotten.

Restoration of the hearth, fireplace, and placement of a damper completed the masonry work. A coat of paint on the floor and this room was ready for a new owner.

THE REAR OF THE HOUSE

After the installation of the back stairs, it seemed best to consider that upstairs room as a sitting room, library, or TV room because, with the invasion of the stairs, it was no longer private. This room also accessed the attic.

From here a corridor led to a bedroom at the opposite end of the house. Off this corridor was the second floor bathroom in the same space as it originally was found. We installed a new cast iron tub and a pine vanity. A fan and a heat lamp were installed in the ceiling. Throughout the second floor we used old-fashioned sconces and lanterns from the Federal Street Lighthouse.

The most rewarding find in this part of the house was that every single interior wall was lined with feather-edged sheathing beneath the Victorian lath and plaster. As we excavated wall after wall, we found the sheathing everywhere we looked. Best of all, it had never been painted. The old plaster was removed throughout this area and the sheathing emerged to be cleaned up and admired after being hidden for maybe one hundred and fifty years.

Just when we thought we were finished and all was in readiness for marketing, I noticed as I came down the attic stairs that the wall beside me was wood. Why wasn't it plastered? The outside of the wall was plastered and already redecorated. Could this be more sheathing? Had we not discovered all of it?

More sheathing it was. The plaster was pulled down and the sheathing restored. This time it really was the end. All the ancient pine had been revealed. The house had given up its last secret.

THE BEDRAGGLED BARN

There was not much positive that could be said about the barn. It was frail, it was rotten, and two stories tall. There were two bays on the first floor and an appendage because the barn was not deep enough for a car. It seemed best to restore the front as intended and add a few feet onto the rear of the building to satisfy the need for more depth.

Inside the door on the left was a steep flight of stairs leading to the upstairs.

This old barn, however, did have some history. The upstairs contained bits and pieces of leather. We soon discovered a chapter of area history.

In the 19th century, Lynn developed as the center of the shoe industry. This shoe industry soon provided winter work for area farmers. This is how it worked.

Agents or couriers from the shoe company called "bag men" fanned out across the region, perhaps as far as Portsmouth, with bags of raw materials for local cordwainers who would complete a certain part of the production. The bag men would return after a certain length of time to pick up the completed work and drop off a new bag of raw material. The finished product would be taken to Lynn for completion and assembly. The shoes were then shipped all over the country.

Many cordwainers had a small building dedicated to this purpose. Some were shared with a neighbor or relative. These little buildings were complete with a stove or, if particularly early, a fireplace, paneled doors, and simple finishes. They were of nice proportions and some were architectural gems. The nickname for these little buildings was "a ten-footer," representing the average size. Although they varied slightly. Time has taken its toll. Few remain. All are dilapidated and may not even be identified. Many were located in the Ipswich and Rowley area. Ipswich Village was the heart of the cordwainer cottage industry.

Amos Jewett was one such cordwainer. He sold the Jewett property to Daniel Boynton in several stages between 1835 and 1844. Daniel Boynton was also a cordwainer. If the Jewetts had "a ten-footer," it does not remain, but they did have a barn with a nice second floor for a shop. Apparently, the second floor became the center of this operation, judging by the evidence left behind.

It is obvious that there was once a bigger barn on the farm. What we are referring to as a barn was probably just an accessory building when this was a working farm. The only other notable issue with the barn was how it got a big hole in the floor (more later) and the miracle that it was saved and still upright.

PART THREE

FINISHED AT LAST

PARTY TIME

Still in very high spirits, we planned a big open house and party by invitation. We were so ambitious, we decided to bring appointments from our own homes and collections to adorn the house. We had a really big toy and we wanted to play house with it. By the day of the party we had essentially furnished the house, if only for a short time.

I brought my dining room chairs and rug for the dining room. My blue velvet wing chair would go in the parlor with its blue woodwork along with my blue Chinese rug and my mother's tilt-top table that our handy man had just refinished for me; also my tea table that I had purchased from my friend, Jane Nelson, from Newburyport. In the old kitchen would be my old pine box chair by the fireplace.

The working kitchen had room for my Windsor and banister-back chairs and my old scale, and some of my dolls would look great in the loft. My treasured washstand was between the twin beds and a cute diminutive bench was at the foot of the stairs along with my small oriental rug.

Nancy's reproduction canopy bed was upstairs in the guest bedroom. My friend, Noel, came from Connecticut to help me sew a new set of bed hangings in unbleached muslin for the bed. My mother's one-drawer stand was next to the bed. David supplied oriental rugs.

Donn Pollard brought Sheraton fancy chairs for the guest bed chamber and an antique portrait for the parlor. He also brought a washstand for the guest room, a wing chair for the upstairs sitting room, and a candelabra for the parlor.

Our handyman supplied the dining room table, a wonderful mirror with a reverse painting, and some small items. Bob Molinski contributed antique rope twin beds and quilts.

Yolanda Martin brought her pewter collection and portraits to go above the twin beds. More than that, Yolanda offered to make window treatments. Nellie and I found remnants of material at the Handkerchief Factory in Exeter, New Hampshire. And Yolanda did the sewing. All the windows were draped with toile, stripes, small prints, and unbleached muslin. It was an admirable selection of attractive window coverings.

The ever practical Yolanda also thought to bring soap, towels, waste baskets, and other necessities for the party.

Only the dining room was left without window treatments. At the last minute, the night before the party, I whipped up simple swags using rich ivory antique satin.

Sometime earlier, I had noticed a Chinese Chippendale camel-back loveseat at Bob's shop. It was pretty awful. It was covered in a disgusting pink material. In lieu of welting, it had black fringe. The wood and fretwork was painted black. I decided that it had more potential than anyone realized and decided to buy it. I waited until all the customers had gone. I didn't want to be seen buying this horror.

Nancy stripped the wood trim and stained it a rich mahogany. I found Nellie's favorite "tree of life, bird of paradise" fabric and took the loveseat to Bonnie Kishbaugh in Hampton, New Hampshire, for reupholstering.

On the day of the party, I borrowed David's Jeep and went to Hampton to get the loveseat. It would go into the Moses Jewett house for the party and for a few extra days before being taken to my house in Lanesville. I was thrilled with the outcome. The loveseat was so pleasing, I actually pulled over a couple of times and turned around to admire it in the back of the vehicle as I drove from Hampton to Ipswich.

Back in Ipswich, things were coming together. Ernie and Coralie had arrived from Dalton, the first guests. Ernie helped carry the loveseat into the parlor. Perfect!

Meanwhile, Nancy, home in Gloucester, had a problem with her car. How could she get to Ipswich from Lanesville? In desperation, she decided to thumb. Lady Luck was with her. She was picked up by Bob Hamlin from Walker Creek Furniture, who was on this way to deliver a handmade reproduction pewter cupboard. He agreed to unload it at the house and pick it up after the party. So Nancy arrived with this wonderful cupboard. Into the old kitchen it went and was quickly filled with Yolanda's pewter, just as the guests arrived. Bob Hamlin's business cards were on the shelf.

Fires burned in the fireplaces. The candle chandelier hung over the table. Everything was picture-perfect. We had a house full of admirers from near and far, including all the neighbors: Sue and Steve Stevens from the Aaron Jewett house, Barbara and Wayne King, Hillman and Priscilla Barney, Dorothy Brigham, Edna Jewett, and of course, Nellie and her eccentric husband, Hal. By the end of the day, music was playing. Friends and neighbors alike were dancing in front of the fireplace in the old kitchen. A good time was had by all. The house was launched into its new chapter. Now all we had to do was find a buyer.

INCIDENTS ALONG THE WAY

Summer was still mostly with us when we began this challenging project. Fall came on quickly, however, followed by a long winter. The lovely warm days turned to bone-chilling episodes in the as-yet unheated old house.

There was often a fire in the big fireplace, and I huddled there on an overturned five-gallon joint compound bucket—almost sitting inside the huge fireplace trying to warm up.

David and Tony checked in with the workers regularly. I remember my role as mostly researching solutions and then convincing my partners after I had worked out a problem in my head. They were reasonable and not hard to convince. We worked well together.

Tony unexpectedly announced that he would like to buy the house for himself and his family. I think it must have been a deteriorating real estate market and escalating interest rates that ultimately discouraged him and his wife, and they backed out of the plan to buy.

One day, someone knocked at the front door. I was as surprised to see a Lanesville neighbor standing there as she was to see me on the other side of the threshold. She had been watching the progress and wondered where we had found the bull's eye glass.

Another time, David and I observed two men walking up the driveway toward the house. I freaked! I recognized them as two purist house restorers, and I was scared to death to let them in. What would they think? Of course, we did let them in. They were antiques dealer, Roger Pheulpin, and Attorney Steve Green. They looked around with interest, and if they didn't approve, they kept it to themselves. We became good friends, and I have enjoyed their acquaintance and benefited from their knowledge ever since.

One day, as I drove to Ipswich early in the morning, I saw our handyman going into an Essex antiques shop. He was carrying a small-dog weathervane that had been in our barn. I stopped to see what was going on. He said that the tail on the dog was broken and he was getting it fixed for us. "Thanks," I said and left feeling more than a little disturbed. He had recently been laid up with a badly injured leg because of a fall but was back in circulation.

The real estate office had a call one day from a motorist saying that there was lots of smoke coming from the chimney. Someone went to the house and saw smoke inside. The new oil burner had backfired and left a film on everything. Professionals were called in to clean. It was covered by insurance and turned out okay, but just the thought of having all our work sullied before the house even hit the market was disconcerting.

On one of my regular visits to the house, I headed for the cellar and opened the door. The cellar stairs looked weird or were my eyes playing tricks on me? I was having trouble seeing the stairs. After a few seconds of bewilderment, I came to my senses and realized half of the staircase was underwater! I lowered a long-handled shovel into the water to see how deep it was. When my hand hit the water, I dropped the shovel. I had not hit bottom. The water was that deep! The sump pump had failed. Now I appreciated the wisdom of the old arrangement of trenches around the cellar and the hole in the foundation. All these disasters, and the house had not yet been put on the market.

Eventually, we started having open houses. The house attracted so much interest that many of the Realtors placing the open house sign at the end of the driveway were invariably followed back to the house by a passerby just dying to see it.

The project was highly visible. Several newspapers came for interviews and tours and there was publicity galore. Nellie, our most loyal mentor and decorator, kept coming over the road to follow the progress. The finished product was going to be great.

One Sunday after an open house, we all gathered around the fireplace. It was decided that Bob Fish and David would go to the shore and get mussels and Shelly Martin would cook them. Next to the fireplace was a wonderful large copper pot that had been contributed by Bob Molinski's friend, Michael.

Bob and David returned with the mussels, which Shelley cooked in the copper pot, adding wine and garlic and steaming them on the new Jennair stove. We all sat in the old kitchen awaiting this treat. Suddenly, there was a terrible explosion in the kitchen! Thoroughly startled and scared, we rushed to the kitchen. The copper pot was so big it had hung over the edge of the stove, overlapping the Formica counter. As the mussels steamed, the copper transferred the heat to the counter, the Formica inflated like a big balloon and then blew! A big hole in the counter remained. The damage was ultimately rectified by cutting out that section of the counter and inserting a large cutting board.

Unbeknownst to us, the most dramatic of events was about to begin. We were marketing the house in earnest. The market was not so good. The excitement of discovery and restoration was behind us. So was the party. Open houses and showings were now the order of the day.

After the party, a few appointments were left in the house for varying amounts of time to take the emptiness from the bare rooms. The plan was to gradually remove them when it was convenient, but with no rush to do so.

A new broker, Jackie Cordima, went to the house to meet a buyer shortly after the party. They made a quick phone call to the office. "Pru, did you take your wing chair home? It's not here." I rushed to the house. The wing chair was gone. So was the box chair by the fireplace and the oriental rug that had been in front of the fireplace.

A few days later, Jackie went to the house and called me again. "Pru, your loveseat and tea table are gone." No! Not my wonderful loveseat of which I was so proud. "Tell me it isn't so." But it was. David's rugs were gone as well.

In the ensuing week, the Chinese rug, the bannister-back chair, my mother's tilt-top table, the scale with the brass scoop, and my treasured washstand were added to the list. The police were called again and again until they said something like, "It's that Fish woman again." They didn't seem to be too hot on the trail of a thief. Yolanda, Donn, and the handy man had already removed their things so suffered no loss.

Jackie had discovered so many thefts that she began to think they would be suspecting her, but it wasn't over yet. Once again Jackie made the discovery.

Arriving at the house one day, she tried to enter the back door only to find the Jennair stove lying on its face with the oven door handle broken off. This stove had been built-in and was wrenched from its spot in the kitchen counter and dragged toward the door until the handle gave way and the stove fell over and was subsequently abandoned.

One day, while driving home to Gloucester, I spotted my mother's tilt-top table in front of an antiques shop. Oh, no! The antiques dealer had purchased it from our handyman. Then I remembered the weathervane incident. Our handyman was a thief! He restored my table, then stole it and sold it. How dare he!

Another day, one of his buddies who had helped with the boiler removal said, "Richie really hurt himself when he fell through the barn floor. That was really something." So that's how he hurt his leg! That's when he stole the weathervane! Served him right that he hurt himself, the thief!

This problem was compounded when I discovered that my own house had been robbed. Bob Molinski discovered his antiques shop had also been robbed. We were living in the middle of a nightmare.

To sum it up, the police were ineffective, the court failed to convict. I recovered my mother's table but nothing else. My wing chair, tea table, new loveseat, washstand and so much more were gone for good.

We tried to put this behind us and move on, but panic was setting in. Our interest rate and carrying costs were skyrocketing. We needed a buyer and we needed one fast.

THE FURNITURE

While all the work and other details were being tended to at the house and in the office, Nancy was hard at work on the old Waycott furniture. The pieces most interesting were probably left from Mrs. Waycott's parents, the Eilenbergers, who had lived there before the Waycotts.

Most of it was dismal but some of it saleable, with Nancy's help. The best was in the attic and consisted of Larkin chairs and bureaus. (That oak furniture earned by saving Larkin soap wrappers.) What was thrown away not too many years ago was now in vogue. Pressback chairs could be sold and *were* sold.

In the lean-to, we found the bottom of an old oak sideboard. It was filthy. Oil had spilled on it. Old tools were in the drawers, and remnants of linens had been attacked by mice. It did seem as though it might have possibilities with work. Suddenly, I remembered something under the eaves in the attic. It was the etegere top for the sideboard with what-not shelves and beveled mirror soaring for several feet above the sideboard base. It was a big job to clean and refinish it, but when it was back to its original condition, we took it to Bob's shop, and he put it in the show window with a light on it. It was gone in a day! I can't remember the price, but it may have been $800.

Another gem was a pine cupboard. That went equally fast for similar money. The remainder of the things were so unremarkable that today I can't even recall them, but little by little they were all sold.

Two large sterling serving spoons had an "E" on the handle, probably for Eilenberger. The pattern was Towle Canterbury from the 1890s. I gave these beautiful spoons to the new owners, Hugh and Jerry. I think I kept a doorstop to give to them later on, but that's all I remember keeping.

SUBDIVISION

Distasteful as it was, we had to think about our ace in the hole. We could subdivide and sell off two lots, but we were a little short of the necessary frontage. Our lawyer confided to us that our neighbors, the Barneys, needed to replace their septic system and it might be just the right time to negotiate the purchase of a few feet from them to make the subdivision work. We let our lawyer, George Hayes, do the negotiating. The deal was accepted and completed.

Now we could offer the whole package for $180,000 or the house alone for $150,000. I prayed for a buyer to come along who would want the whole thing. I didn't want to be a party to subdividing. Spring turned to summer and summer to fall. We were more nervous than cats on a hot tin roof. We couldn't give it back to the bank, nor could we continue to carry this huge burden.

One day, a Realtor from our office, Dottie Levesque, said cheerfully, "Pru, I have good news for you. I have an offer for one of the lots." My heart sank. This would bail us out but I had been holding my breath that we wouldn't have to do this. But do it we did. We had no choice. The contract was signed.

In just a few days, another Realtor from the office, Sandra Jervah, took two buyers from New York out to look at properties. She took them all over Rockport and Gloucester. Late in the day, they returned to the office, having not found what they wanted. We were introduced and I chatted with them. They were selling a business in Manhattan and wanted to move to New England.

My brain clicked into gear. They were two people escaping New York City for a taste of New England. What was more New England than our Moses Jewett house sitting there waiting? What could be finer than our picture-perfect Currier and Ives farmhouse in the country?

"Sandra," I said. "Didn't you show them the Moses Jewett house?"

"No," she replied. "I didn't even think of it."

She didn't think of it? Our own office listing! And she had dragged them all over Cape Ann for nothing. I had trouble containing myself and bit my tongue.

I proceeded to tell them about the house, got them excited, gave them the listing material, gave Sandra the key and told her to get them up there on the double. They went and just as I fantasized, they loved it. In fact, they were infatuated with the history, the restoration and everything about it. Better still, they bought it.

We had more heartbreak when they told us they would like all of the land, all six acres. There was nothing we could do. It was under agreement to Dottie's customers and the die was cast. The last of the Jewett farm of 100 acres was now subdivided into three two-acre parcels.

BUYERS AT LAST

On November 17, 1982, the lot on the street east of the house was sold to the Fowlers, who would build a home on the site. The closing on our house was set for December 1st.

At this point David decided he would buy the lot in the rear that would be up a long driveway. His plan was to build a Maine Post and Beam saltbox for himself, Shelley and his boys, Zachary and Spencer. He would sell his house in Newbury but would need a place to live while building.

It turned out that Hugh and Jerry, our buyers from New York, would not be ready to move in until the following summer, so an agreement was reached whereby David and family would live in the Moses Jewett house until their house was completed.

There would be no mortgage or bank involved in the sale, so the closing could take place right there in the house. Hugh and Jerry arrived and we all gathered around a big table in the old kitchen in front of the fireplace. We had wine. A toast was in order. David conducted the closing and tallied up the assorted checks to make up the total selling price. After the closing, David drove Hugh and Jerry to the Registry of Deeds in Salem where the deed was recorded.

Was that the end of the story? Not at all! As work progressed on David's new house with its long driveway, he affectionately called his house "One Post Road" after the name of our group, Post Road Development Corporation, and the historic reference to the old highway called the Post Road.

It was the summer of 1983 when Hugh and Jerry arrived with a truck and moved into the Moses Jewett house. David was in his new house. The Fowlers had a new cape next door. What a lot of change since that September day when we purchased the old place nearly two years earlier.

The first Christmas, 1983, Hugh and Jerry had a party. All of their guests were Realtors from the Vernon A. Martin office. The only people they had met were Realtors, but by now everyone in the office knew them. What a house for a party. Candles, fires in the fireplaces, great food and drink were in abundance. This was the first of many. A pattern emerged. A Christmas party was held each December, usually on a Sunday evening, and another convivial party in the late summer, on the newly built bluestone patio just outside the two back doors. The numbers grew, people came and went. The cast of characters changed, but the routine remains to this day. No one who has ever crossed that threshold can forget the ambiance, the fires, the warm friendships, and good times.

David and Shelley moved on. Their house was sold. The land was further subdivided. Imagine my surprise when driving past the old place one day to see a new street sign on what had previously been David's driveway years before. And what did they name this new street? Post Road Lane! I was incredulous. The inside joke from twenty years before had become a reality and now numerous families make their home on Post Road Lane.

Over fifty years later, Hugh and Jerry, our buyers, are still happily ensconced in the house. The parties continue. The neighbors and friends keep coming. It has been a good half century plus for the old Moses Jewett house.

MISTAKES

Looking back over these years and visiting the house as often as I have, there has been plenty of opportunity to review some of the mistakes and think about what we should or should not have done. Most of my thoughts are positive, without too many regrets.

One dilemma we faced is a common one. The windows were in bad shape. They were not 18th century originals, but they were still old. The glass was good with lots of waviness. In a perfect world it would seem that we should have restored them. We didn't actually think they were restorable. We restored a few to use in the barn and they are once again in collapse. The house started out to be a spec house, not a pure restoration, but early on we knew we must do our best. The windows we chose were wood, true divided light windows, and they have held up perfectly. My regret is losing all that old glass.

It was our dream to put on a cedar roof. The roof on the house was good but not wood. The budget, however, dictated that we had to cross that off the list. The new owners did follow through and put on a wood roof. Unfortunately, it could not breathe and did not last, so the roof is back to architectural shingles. What a pity.

There is one little mistake that haunts me. We did not know at that time that the thumb latches and HL hinges should have been painted the same as the woodwork and made to disappear. We left them black. That will embarrass me forever. I have begged the owners to cover the hinges but they like them as they are. And those jet black hinges still glare back at me.

Initially, we all made the mistake of tearing out the dining room ceiling. First of all, we misjudged what we would find. Secondly, we did not think we were doing any great damage. The plaster was too bad to save, wasn't it? Wrong! As we found out, the worst plaster can be saved. All the rest was saved after that first mistake. I'm proud of the way the plaster looks in the light. Not rough, but slightly undulating. It's just right. I'm so glad we were stopped before we took down more than we did.

Finishing the floors in a natural finish was probably a good idea, not knowing who our buyer would be. They can always be painted but the only one that has been is the kitchen.

The skylights, questionable to a purist, have been good for light and air. I don't regret installing them nor do I regret the eyeball lights in the dining room that shocked people back then. Hugh and Jerry replaced the stolen chandelier with a wonderful antique brass chandelier for candles. The eyeball lights on a dimmer supplement the candles perfectly. I don't consider these modern touches a mistake by any means.

On the lighter side, while cleaning for an open house, Tony learned that you cannot vacuum a hearth when its bricks are set in sand.

After vehemently resisting using the term "borning room," a misnomer from the colonial revival period, I fell into the same sort of trap. It was common back then for restorers to call the old kitchen the "keeping room." I'm not sure where this came from, but we went along with it. Later I realized this was less than accurate. I have only seen that term on one old house plan. It was from the Federal period and it pertained to a sitting room. I have since ceased to ever use the term but the damage was done. Everyone associated with the restoration, and especially the new owners, have never failed to refer to the colonial kitchen with the big fireplace as the keeping room, a term of which I am sorry I ever heard or uttered. It is corny. I know better now, but it's too late. The term refuses to go away.

When all is said and done, I think it is miraculous that we did as good a job as we did. Looking back, I think we were naïve about the project, but we did our homework, tried hard to get it right, and absolutely did the best we could.

Did we make mistakes? Sure, but most could be reversed and none were too serious or resulted in permanent damage.

CONCLUSIONS

The lesson learned from this experience is that restoring an old house is exciting and fun, as long as:

- You hire contractors
- It is not a spec
- You have deep pockets (a must!)
- Someone checks every day to catch mistakes early on
- Originality is respected
- You don't try to make it into something it isn't
- You are pro-active and do your homework
- You seek advice from professionals
- The family isn't trying to live there during construction

My rules for restoration, evolved through this experience, are these:

1. Accommodate the old house and its floor plan. Do not try to make the house accommodate you.
2. Do not remove original fabric. Plaster can be saved. Horse hair is not bad!
3. Do not do anything that can't be reversed.

POST SCRIPT ON POST ROAD

It is now 2021. There has been a lot of water under the bridge, but the Moses Jewett house is still going strong. Hugh and Jerry are retired but still there. Next week is Thanksgiving 2021, and I will be at the Thanksgiving feast in the old kitchen in front of the big fireplace. It has been forty years since the day I agreed to become part of the Moses Jewett house team. Everyone involved with the house is much older, the cast of characters has changed, and some have passed on, including Bob Molinski, Nellie, Vern Martin, and the thieving handy man. Everyone has fond memories of the house and the hospitality of Hugh and Jerry.

It will soon be Christmas and New Year's Eve again. The front of the house is decorated. Once again I expect to be a dinner guest for an elegant New Year's Eve dinner in the dining room, under the chandelier with candles and with Nellie's tree-of-life-bird-of-paradise wallpaper still on the walls.

May the good times in the olde house at Ipswich Village never end!

Bonus Chapter

THANKSGIVING IN IPSWICH

This year, as in other years, I will enjoy my Thanksgiving dinner in the perfect setting; a red 18th century country farmhouse. No, it is not my house. It's the Moses Jewett house, located in Ipswich Village Massachusetts, near the Rowley line. Built in 1759, it is the oldest of a string of Jewett houses along Old Post Road, all of them ancient and all representing different generations of the Jewett family. One, or perhaps two, even earlier houses are no longer standing. The location of the earliest known Jewett house is quite some distance from this house near

the Egypt River. There has been a suggestion that perhaps another house existed closer to this one, but I am not aware of any concrete evidence.

My acquaintance with this old house goes back to the 1980s when I was a partner in a restoration project involving the house and a barn out back. It was originally intended to be just a quick-fixer-upper, but as soon as we owned it we knew it was a serious antique and we had to do it right. With that revelation came the realization there would be no profits with this "quick-fixer-upper."

Was I sorry? Not at all! The experience of uncovering, evaluating what we had, and making the decisions that were necessary to be made, taught me more about old houses than I could possibly have known otherwise. We started out as spec buyers, but this unexpected exercise in preservation turned us into restoration purists.

We made some mistakes, but looking back on the project in its entirety, I think we did fairly well. The project was complicated by the fact that we knew we would end up selling the house, so we tried to keep in mind various scenarios for appealing to a cross-section of buyers.

One of our best decisions was keeping the kitchen and the first floor bath/laundry in a lean-to that was 19th century but not very significant. This kept the old part of the house free of modern intrusions. We kept a small upstairs bath where it had always been, rather than rip out walls to change it. Sometimes accommodating an old house can mean eliminating the idea of extravagant bathrooms and kitchens. As you know by now, I am always talking about accommodating the house instead of trying to make the old house accommodate you when it means ripping out walls and original fabric.

The house had an exterior door in the Beverly jog that was not going to be used. The laundry and first floor bath were planned for the other side of the door. Our solution was to leave the door intact. The wall on the inside was sheetrocked and plastered and no evidence of this door remained on the interior. We gained the wall space we needed but the door is still there if sometime down the road someone has a different plan for this space. In other words, what we did is easily reversed. No original fabric was lost or even jeopardized.

Several floors had to be replaced. The original floors were painted as they had long been, but we stained the floors we replaced knowing that refinished pine floors are popular and would appeal to some buyers, while the old worn floors with paint would be acceptable to another group of buyers.

We ripped out one terrible looking ceiling before we were stopped in our tracks by our contractor. That's when we found out that all of those ugly, peeling ceilings could be saved without loss of any more original plaster. Initially, I thought the ceilings resembled lumpy oatmeal. They were so rough I never dreamed they could be saved. (Important lesson learned: Don't rip out the plaster and lath. It is original fabric and can be saved.)

A common mistake is leaving the hinges and thumb latches black. These should have been painted to match the woodwork and made to disappear. They shouldn't stand out. Black hardware is "phony colonial," but that's what we did. I know better now.

The new windows should have had heavier muntins. We knew this, but it just wasn't in the budget.

So now, many years later, I think many of our decisions were tough decisions and I still feel good about most of the things we did.

Anyway, we sold the house to people from New York City looking for a taste of New England. This house was perfect; just what they were looking for. The closing was conducted at a big table in front of the fireplace in the old kitchen with a fire burning. This was followed by a trip to the Registry of Deeds to record the deed. It was hardly the traditional closing taking place in a lawyer's office.

It has worked out well. I have been a frequent guest back in the old house ever since. My family is not nearby, so the owners always make sure I have an invitation for the holidays if they know my family won't be around. In addition to holiday dinners, a small group of friends has celebrated New Year's Eve in the old house ever since our buyers took up residence.

Often, there are others in attendance who have no idea I had anything to do with the restoration. So I quietly listen to the reaction of the newer attendees who are in awe of the ambiance of the house, decorated for the holidays with fires in the fireplaces, especially the fireplace in the old kitchen that approaches ten feet in width.

It seems as though the house was built just for the holidays. It is the quintessential Currier and Ives "Home to Thanksgiving" kind of house.

Home to Thanksgiving
(Currier & Ives Lithograph, 1860)

Reprinted from:

Curious Stories of Old New England
By
Prudence Paine Fish

© 2022 by Prudence Paine Fish

More From Prudence Paine Fish

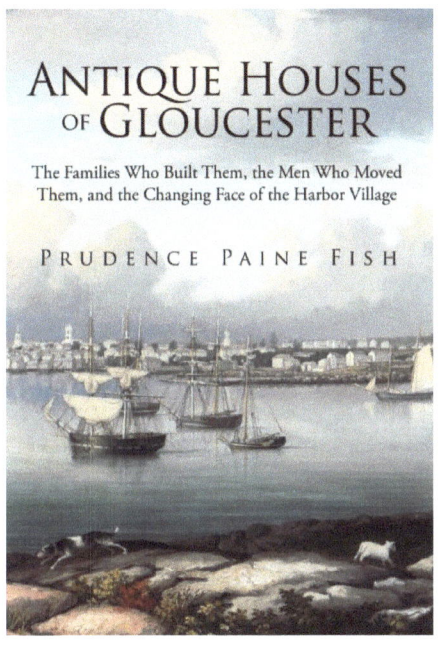

Available at all fine bookstores & Amazon

www.ingramcontent.com/pod-product-compliance
Lightning Source LLC
Chambersburg PA
CBHW040053160426
43192CB00002B/61